5755 7471

W9-ALW-048

THE SICKENING HISTORY OF MEDICINE

Tiny Killers

WHEN BACTERIA AND VIRUSES ATTACK

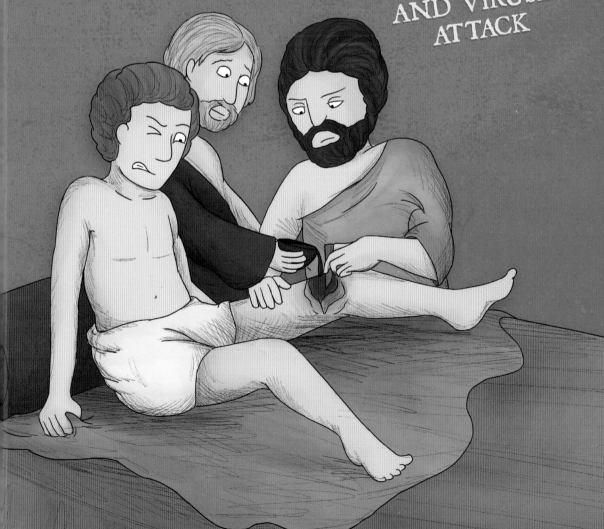

Thanks to the creative team:
Senior Editor: Alice Peebles
Editor: Angela Koo
Fact Checker: Kate Mitchell
Design: www.collaborate.agency

Hungry Tomato™
A division of Lerner Publishing Group, Inc.
241 First Avenue North
Minneapolis, MN 55401 USA

For reading levels and more information, look up this title at
www.lernerbooks.com.

Main body text set in Futura Std Book, 11/14.
Typeface provided by Adobe Systems.

Library of Congress Cataloging-in-Publication Data

Names: Farndon, John, author. | Dean, Venitia, 1976–
illustrator.
Title: Tiny killers : when bacteria and viruses attack / John
Farndon ; illustrated by Venitia Dean.
Description: Minneapolis : Hungry Tomato, [2017] | Series:
The sickening history of medicine | Audience: Ages 8–12. |
Audience: Grades 4 to 6. | Includes index.
Identifiers: LCCN 2016025300 (print) | LCCN 2016028071
(ebook) | ISBN 9781512415582 (lb : alk. paper) | ISBN
9781512430783 (pb : alk. paper) | ISBN 9781512427103 (eb
pdf)
Subjects: LCSH: Diseases—Causes and theories of
causation—Juvenile literature. | Germ theory of disease—
Juvenile literature. | Medicine—History—Juvenile literature.
Classification: LCC RB153 .F37 2017 (print) | LCC RB153
(ebook) | DDC 616.009—dc23

LC record available at https://lccn.loc.gov/2016025300

Manufactured in the United States of America
1-39918-21388-8/16/2016

THE SICKENING HISTORY OF MEDICINE

Tiny Killers

By John Farndon
Illustrated by Venitia Dean

HUNGRY TOMATO

Contents

INTRODUCTION

Germs are tiny organisms, or living things, that make you sick. Because they're far too small to see, they sneak into your body without you noticing and then infect you with all kinds of terrible diseases. But over time, these microscopic monsters were finally unmasked . . .

Home Wreckers

Germs don't actually try to make us sick. It's just that bodies like ours make very good homes for them, and once they get inside, they multiply rapidly to make the most of their good luck! That's how they do the damage.

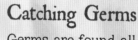

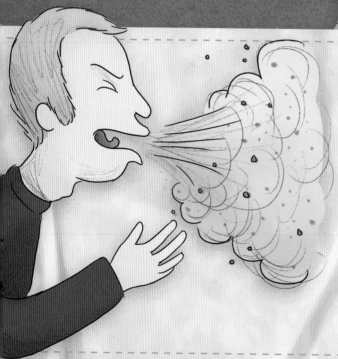

Catching Germs

Germs are found all over the world, in all kinds of places. Some reach you through the air from sneezes, coughs, or someone's breath. You can also become infected if you touch something contaminated with germs, then touch your nose and breathe in. Other germs can be swallowed when you eat bad food.

Defenders

Luckily, your body has an amazing defense system for dealing with germs called the immune system. It's a complex army of tiny cells that circulate in your blood and do battle with germs. It often takes time to kick in though. That's why you get ill—then, with luck, recover because your immune system has dealt with them.

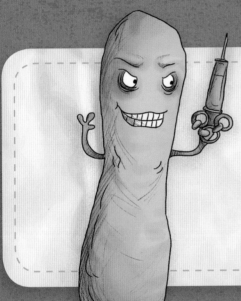

Doctor's Orders

Doctors have two ways of helping your body fight germs. One is with vaccination, which gets your immune system ready to fight certain germs. The other is with antibiotics—medicine that is poisonous to germs.

Keeping Clean

There's another way we can reduce the danger of germs—by cleanliness, or hygiene. Many germs spread in dirt, so by keeping things clean, we reduce the chances of infection. That's why it's good to wash your hands.

SETTLING FOR GERMS

In the early days of mankind, when people roamed around hunting and gathering, infectious diseases were probably rare. People did not live close enough together for germs to spread or stay long enough near water sources to pollute them.

Disease on the Farm

The development of farming some ten thousand years ago saved mankind from starvation and provided food for the first towns and cities. But germs multiplied as people and farm animals began living close together, sharing their germs and polluting the water.

Slow-moving water provided a breeding ground for parasites.

Cattle gave us tuberculosis and smallpox.

Dogs gave us measles.

Chickens may have given us flu.

The First Known Polio Victim?

On an Egyptian monument from the thirteenth century BCE, there is a picture of a man called Roma. His leg seems to be withered, which could be caused by polio. If so, he is the first known victim of this terrible disease, which may have developed in water dirtied by the dung of farm animals.

As farming became more intense, manure-polluted water encouraged diseases such as polio, cholera, typhoid, and hepatitis. Slow-moving irrigation water provided ideal conditions for parasites such as those causing the diseases bilharzia and malaria.

Horses gave us the common cold.

Polio may have developed in water dirtied by farm animal dung.

Pigs may have given us flu.

9

BAD AIR

Few people had any idea diseases were spread by tiny invisible germs. Most thought bad, smelly air was to blame—especially damp, misty air near ditches and swamps. This nasty mist was called a miasma.

Dealing with Odors

Most people in ancient India, and elsewhere in the world, thought disease was caused by poisonous air. They chewed a paste made from the leaves of the gambir tree as an antidote.

Morning Smells

The Roman writer Vitruvius thought that it was a bad idea to build a city near a swamp. He believed the wind would blow miasmas, along with the poisonous breath of swamp creatures, from the swamp to the city and make people ill.

Taking it on the Ch'in

Government officials in ancient China knew they were in trouble if they were sent off to the south! The Ch'in Mountains there were damp and misty, and people were convinced that poisonous air would make them get sick and die.

Smoke in New Orleans

The city of New Orleans often suffered from outbreaks of disease. People thought this was because of air full of evil spirits coming from the nearby swamps. They burned bonfires of feverfew plants and fired cannons into the air to keep the mist away.

The Great Stink

So much sewage once poured into the River Thames in London that in the hot summer of 1858, the stink coming off it was bad enough to make you throw up. They called it the Great Stink, and people began to leave the city, convinced that the terrible smell of sewage gas caused disease. To solve the problem, London built the first modern sewage system.

Taking drinking water from the river could be deadly.

EASTERN IDEAS

You might think people had no idea about germs in the past because they are just too small to see. But in India more than 2,500 years ago, those who followed the Jainist religion were taught that tiny life forms called nigoda existed all around them.

Saving Germs

Just as people often wear surgical masks in order not to breathe in germs, so did the Jains, thousands of years ago. But their aim was not to avoid disease. They believed they must not harm any living thing and wanted to avoid killing the tiny nigoda by accidentally swallowing them!

Ancient Medicine

Ayurveda is an ancient medical system, developed in India more than three thousand years ago, that uses complex mixes of herbs to treat people. Ayurvedists believed more than two thousand years ago that microbes cause diseases such as leprosy and meningitis.

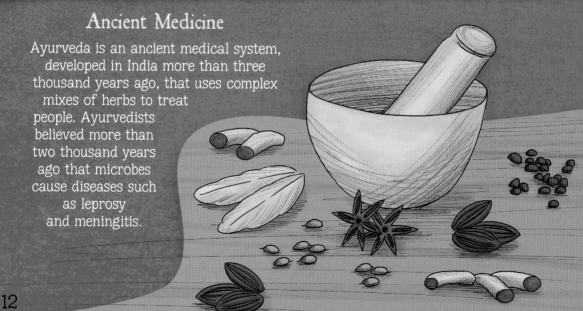

Prevention Better than Cure

The most famous old book of Ayurvedic medicine was the *Charaka Samhita*, written about 2,200 years ago by Charaka. He argued that prevention is better than cure. That's why he suggested different diets to keep people healthy in different places and at different times of the year.

The Plague in Granada

In 1350, the bubonic plague reached Granada in Spain, then part of the Islamic world. Physician Ibn Khatima suggested it was spread by "minute bodies," which sound like germs. Another physician, al-Khatib—shown in the orange headscarf with the Vizier (ruler) in Granada's Alhambra Palace—explained how such organisms spread the plague by contact between people.

INVISIBLE ANIMALS

Around 1590 Dutch glasses maker Zacharias Janssen put some lenses together—and invented the microscope. When people began to look through it, they were amazed by what they saw: a whole new unknown world of tiny organisms, too small to see normally.

Hooked In

In 1665, the English physicist Robert Hooke (1635–1703) published *Micrographia*, a book full of drawings of the amazing things he viewed through a microscope—things people had never seen before. In slices of cork, he could see a honeycomb network of boxes. He called the boxes cells, and people began to understand that all living things are made up of tiny cells.

Tiny Monsters

Dutch scientist Anton van Leeuwenhoek (1632–1723) made a microscope with just a single lens. It was simple but brilliant, and he could see things 200 times larger than life! He discovered that clear water is not clear at all but teeming with tiny creatures. In fact, there are tiny creatures almost everywhere.

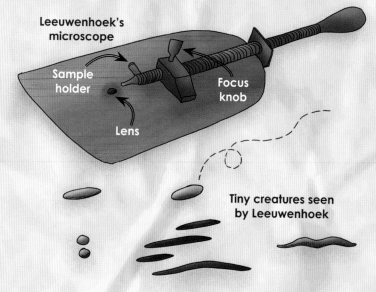

Leeuwenhoek's microscope

Sample holder

Focus knob

Lens

Tiny creatures seen by Leeuwenhoek

Germs Spotted

Leeuwenhoek was astonished by the range of creatures he saw (*above*). It was Leeuwenhoek who saw germs for the first time when he looked through his microscope at the bacteria in plaque taken from teeth.

The Bacteria Four

After Leeuwenhoek's great discovery, no one paid much attention to bacteria for the next two hundred years until German biologist Ferdinand Cohn began to study them closely in the 1870s. Cohn realized that, though there are many kinds of bacteria, they can be divided into four groups depending on their shape: spheres, rods, threads, and spirals.

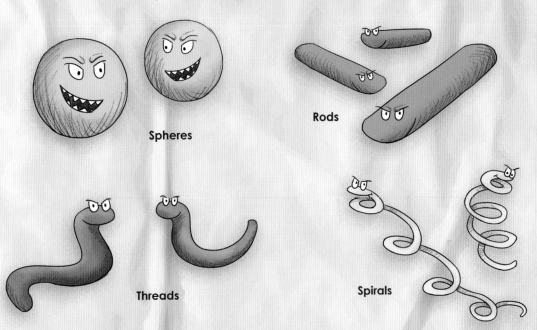

Spheres

Rods

Threads

Spirals

NOW WASH YOUR HANDS

Hospitals in the past were deadly dangerous! Very few people knew that germs caused disease, so doctors and nurses spread diseases as they went from patient to patient, with terrible consequences.

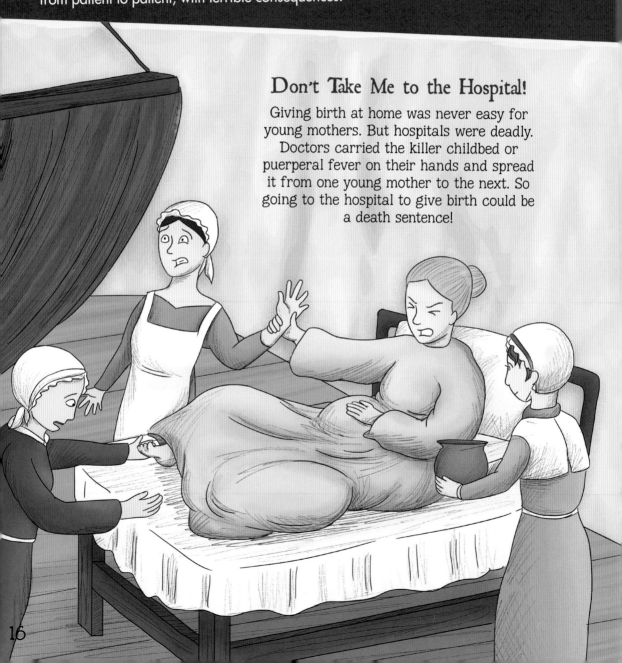

Don't Take Me to the Hospital!

Giving birth at home was never easy for young mothers. But hospitals were deadly. Doctors carried the killer childbed or puerperal fever on their hands and spread it from one young mother to the next. So going to the hospital to give birth could be a death sentence!

The Real Culprit

Of course, the doctors weren't really to blame. Their unwashed hands were simply carrying the germs that were the real culprits. The germ that causes childbed fever is the bacterium *Streptococcus pyogenes*. Fortunately, proper hygiene in hospitals means this germ very rarely has its evil way!

Trust Me, I'm a Doctor!

In Vienna General Hospital in the 1800s, doctors often handled diseased corpses in the mortuary, then went next door to the maternity ward to examine mothers-to-be—with fatal results. When the young Hungarian doctor Ignaz Semmelweis arrived in 1847, he was appalled by the high death rate on the ward—and realized the unwashed hands were to blame.

My Hands are Clean

Semmelweis ordered all medical staff to wash their hands regularly in calcium chloride. At once, death rates in the maternity ward dropped. But doctors could not believe the deaths were their fault. They fired Semmelweis and carried on as before. It was a while before everyone realized just how important hygiene is in stopping germs from spreading.

DIRTY DRAINS

In the 1800s, London and other European cities grew rapidly—and so did deaths from the killer disease cholera. Poor people were especially hard hit by cholera.

Feeling Blue

Cholera is a disease that may have started in India. Victims may suffer from diarrhea so severe that their bodies are drained of water. Their eyes go hollow, their skin shrivels, and they turn blue.

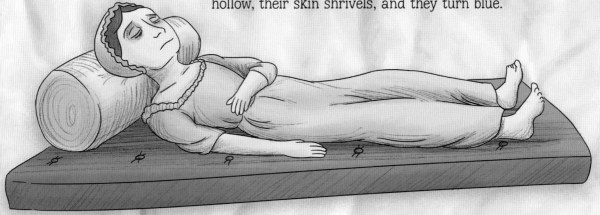

Where's that Smell?

Experts in the past were convinced that cholera was spread by miasmas. So the upper class thought it was obviously smelly poor people who were to blame! A cartoon of the time made fun of health officials trying to sniff out just where the worst stinks were coming from.

The Soho Pump

English doctor John Snow didn't think the miasma theory was right. When cholera hit London's Soho district in 1854, he found that all the victims had drunk water from just one pump on Broadwick Street. Human waste had contaminated the water supply for the pump. But it was a while before people understood that cholera is caused by germs in dirty water.

The Fast Way to Travel

The opening of Egypt's Suez Canal in 1869 cut the sea journey from India to Europe dramatically—and made it much easier for cholera epidemics to spread. London escaped the worst because by then it had built good sewers, but many other European cities suffered badly.

Vicious *Vibrio*

In 1854, cholera hit Florence, in Italy. In Florence, Dr. Filippo Pacini looked through his microscope and identified the culprit: the bacterium *Vibrio cholerae*. But everyone ignored him since they thought miasmas were to blame. Then in 1884, German doctor Robert Koch also nailed *Vibrio* as the cause of cholera. He was so famous that everyone believed him!

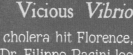

GUILTY GERMS

In the 1840s and 1850s, Semmelweis and Snow showed how clean hands and good drains could cut the spread of disease, so how could bad air be to blame? Then in the 1860s, the French microbiologist Louis Pasteur began to demonstrate that the real culprits are germs, also known as microbes.

Life from Nothing

When people saw maggots on rotten food, they didn't know that the maggots had hatched from eggs. They thought maggots just appeared when food rotted. The idea of life appearing from nothing is known as spontaneous generation.

Life from the Air

In 1859 Pasteur showed that microbes don't appear by spontaneous generation when food decays. Instead, they fall from the air in dust.

1. Pasteur boiled meat broth in a flask with a bent "swan" neck to kill off any microbes.

2. The swan neck stopped dust falling in, so the broth stayed clear.

3. He then broke off the neck to allow dust to fall in. The broth quickly went cloudy, showing microbes were multiplying.

Germs on Worms

In 1867 Pasteur showed that germs can cause disease. He had been studying a disease that was killing silkworms. When Pasteur examined the diseased worms through his microscope, he found they were infected by not just one kind of microbe but two.

Chicken Test

In 1880 Pasteur discovered how to protect people against germs with experiments on chickens. He grew chicken cholera germs in a dish, then starved them of nutrition so they became weak. When he injected chickens with these old germs, the chickens became immune to the disease. Vaccinating people with weakened germs is now one of the main ways of preventing diseases.

Sheep Shot

In 1881 Pasteur also found a way to weaken the germs that cause anthrax in sheep. Using these weak germs, he vaccinated sheep so that they became immune to anthrax.

GERMS NAILED

Louis Pasteur proved there are germs, or microbes, in the air and that they can cause disease. Then Robert Koch showed that there's a whole army of nasty microbes out there—and that it's these nasty microbes that are to blame for most diseases.

Guilty!

In 1876 Koch proved that bacteria can cause disease. He took the bacterium *Bacillus anthracis* from the blood of a sheep that had died of anthrax. Then he injected the bacteria into a mouse. The mouse died of anthrax too, proving that the bacteria caused the disease.

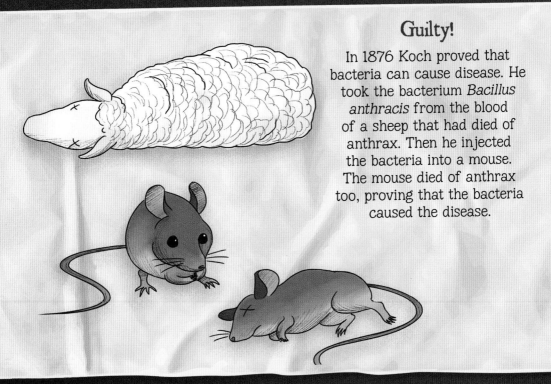

The Criminal

Bacillus anthracis is a rod-shaped organism. It's so tiny you can only see it under a microscope. But despite its small size, it can kill a sheep or even a person. It does its damage by multiplying dramatically in the body and releasing a poison.

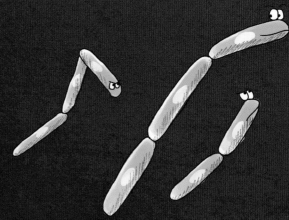

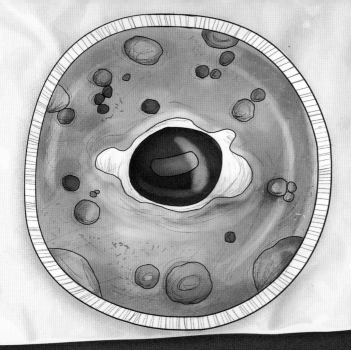

Cultured Germs

For his work, Koch grew germs in a dish in a laboratory. Growths like this are called cultures. At first, Koch used the liquid from an ox's eye as food for germ cultures. Later he developed a broth of agar (a jelly made from algae) and gelatine (a jelly made from animal bones).

The Four Tests

Koch's work led him to establish four tests for proving which germ causes a disease.

1. Association: the germ and the disease are seen together all the time.

2. Isolation: the germ can be taken from the diseased animal and grown in a culture.

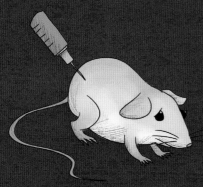

3. Inoculation: the germ taken from the diseased animal causes the disease in a healthy animal.

4. Re-isolation: the germ can also be taken from the newly infected animal.

CLEAN SURGERY

If germs cause disease, how do we stop them? One answer is to keep clean. Semmelweis showed how important it was to keep clean when mothers gave birth. British surgeon Joseph Lister showed that it was also important for surgery.

Mummy, You're Rotten

Dead bodies rot away because they are attacked by microbes. But the Ancient Egyptians learned how to stop the rot by turning the bodies into mummies. This meant soaking the body in embalming fluids that were poisonous to microbes.

Pus is Bad

The thirteenth-century surgeon Hugh of Lucca realized the dangers of wounds becoming infected, so he cleaned them with wine. He knew that pus oozing from a wound was a sign that the wound was infected. Most doctors at the time wrongly thought that pus was a sign that the wound was getting better.

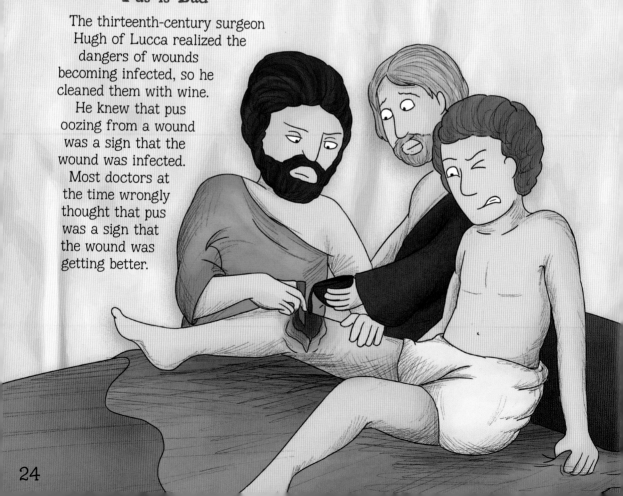

Filth

The growing cities of the 1800s were filthy places because they had no garbage collection, a poor water supply, and a lack of good drains. This meant germs could spread easily. Hospitals were some of the worst culprits for filth!

Clean Surgery

Until the 1860s, many patients undergoing surgery died of infections afterward. Then Joseph Lister (1827–1912) introduced the idea of antiseptic surgery. He made sure that hands, surgical tools, and surfaces 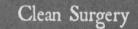 were thoroughly washed with germ-killing chemicals such as carbolic soap. The idea worked and became standard practice around the world.

Masked Doctors

Lister's antiseptic methods stopped the spread of germs from surface to surface. But germs could still spread through the air. The answer was simple—surgeons and other surgical staff needed to wear masks to keep the germs in their breath from infecting patients.

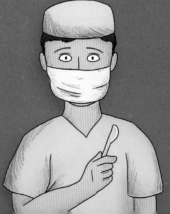

GERM ARMY

Although ninety-nine percent of microbes are completely harmless, scientists have identified about 1,500 that can make you ill. They call these disease-causing microbes pathogens. The main kinds are viruses, fungi, protozoa, and bacteria. Here is a round-up of some of these tiny villains.

Viruses

Viruses are much tinier than any other kind of germ. They only come to life once they have invaded and taken over a living cell, such as one of your body cells.

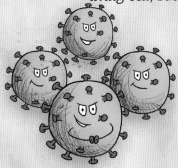

Influenza viruses give you colds and flu. Type C gives you minor colds, type B gives you winter flu, and type A gives you bird flu.

The togavirus causes rubella (German measles).

Adenoviruses give sore throats, colds, bronchitis, conjunctivitis, diarrhea, and pneumonia.

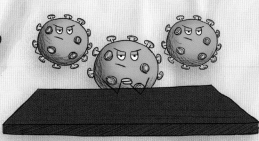

The human immuno-deficiency virus (HIV) causes AIDS.

Fungi and Protozoa

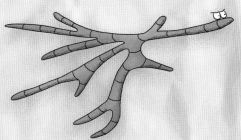

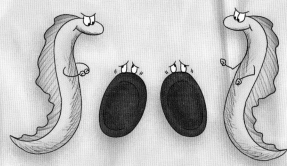

The protozoa *Trypanosoma brucei* causes sleeping sickness by attacking red blood cells.

Fungi can cause skin infections such as athlete's foot.

Bacteria

Bacteria are tiny microbes made from just one cell. Most are harmless, but a few are germs that make you ill.

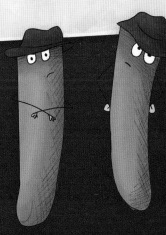

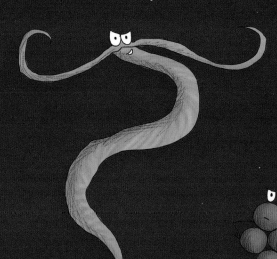

Bacilli are long, thin, and rod-like and cause tetanus (lockjaw), typhoid, tuberculosis (TB), whooping cough, and diphtheria. Not welcome!

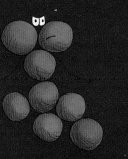

Spirilla look like tiny spiral pasta noodles and cause diarrhea and nausea.

Cocci are round bacteria that cause strep throat, pneumonia, scarlet fever, and meningitis.

GERMY TIMES

Some people suspected that germs caused disease long ago. Here are some of the key steps on the way to the discovery of just what germs are and how they make you ill.

1665
Microscopic Cells

English scientist Robert Hooke saw through a microscope that living things are made from tiny boxes, or cells.

500 CE

1600

Around 1000 BCE
Old Herbalists

In India, the Ayurvedic system of medicine suggested that many diseases were caused by tiny microbes.

1546
The Seeds of Disease

Italian physician Girolamo Fracastoro suggested that diseases are spread by tiny seeds.

1676
Viewing Bacteria

Dutch scientist Anton van Leeuwenhoek was the first person to see bacteria, through a homemade microscope.

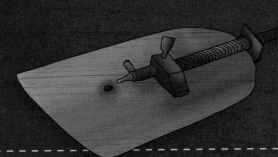

1847 Hygiene

Hungarian doctor Ignaz Semmelweis cut dangerous infections among mothers giving birth simply by getting all medical staff to wash their hands.

1859 Germs in the Air

French scientist Louis Pasteur proved that there are microbes in the air that might cause disease.

1870s Antiseptic Surgery

Surgeon Joseph Lister showed how keeping surgery completely clean kept germs from spreading and patients from dying of infections after surgery.

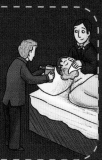

1750   1860

1876 Germs Cause Disease

German doctor Robert Koch proved that a certain bacterium caused the disease anthrax.

1854 Sanitation

London doctor John Snow showed that cholera was spread not by bad vapors but by contaminated water.

1890s Germ Theory

Building on Koch's ideas, scientists developed the germ theory, the idea that a few micro-organisms, known as pathogens or germs, cause all infectious diseases.

GRUESOME SYMPTOMS

One species of bacterium is so resistant to radiation that scientists have nicknamed it Conan the Bacterium.

When you cough, germs can travel about 10 feet (3 meters) if you don't cover your nose or mouth with your hand or a handkerchief.

There are more bacteria on your skin than there are people in the world. Take out the water, and one-tenth of your body weight is bacteria.

Bacteria in your nose and mouth are what give you bad breath.

Poop, by weight, is mostly bacteria.

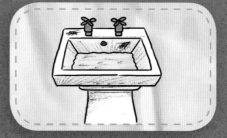

The average kitchen sink contains 100,000 times more germs than the bathroom.

Bacteria double in number every 20 minutes. A single bacterium could divide and multiply into trillions in just one day if all the bacteria survived.

Some soldiers in the American Civil War had glow-in-the-dark wounds because of a bioluminescent bacteria from nematode worms.

When you flush a toilet, an invisible cloud of water full of germs shoots far up into the air.

GLOSSARY

antidote	a remedy for counteracting the effects of a poison or a germ
antiseptic	a substance wiped or sprayed on surfaces to kill germs
Ayurveda	an ancient medical system developed in India that treats people using complex mixes of herbs
bacterium	a very small living thing made from just a single cell. A few of them cause disease. *Bacteria* is the plural of *bacterium*.
bubonic plague	a dreadful disease caused by the *Yersinia pestis* bacterium that often causes distinctive buboes (blisters)
epidemic	a widespread outbreak of an infectious disease
germ	a microbe that causes disease when it enters the body
hygiene	cleanliness that reduces the spread of infection
immune system	the body's microscopic defenses against germs
inoculation	the use of germs to stimulate the body's immune system to guard against infection
miasma	a damp, smelly mist that was believed to spread disease
microbe	a microscopic living thing, especially one that causes diseases
puerperal fever	a disease that affects mothers giving birth, also known as childbed fever
vaccination	the use of dead or inactive germs to stimulate the body's immune system to guard against infection
virus	a tiny germ that reproduces only inside other living cells —including yours

Index

The Author

John Farndon is the author of many books on science, technology, and nature, including the international best sellers *Do Not Open* and *Do You Think You're Clever?* He has been shortlisted six times for the British Royal Society's Young People's Book Prize for a science book.

The Illustrator

Venitia Dean grew up in Brighton, in the United Kingdom. She has loved drawing ever since she could hold a pencil. After receiving a digital drawing tablet for her nineteenth birthday, she began working digitally. She hasn't looked back since!